W9-AIB-749

Contents

A tractor is
a machine
that pulls
heavy loads.

Most tractors
are used
on farms.

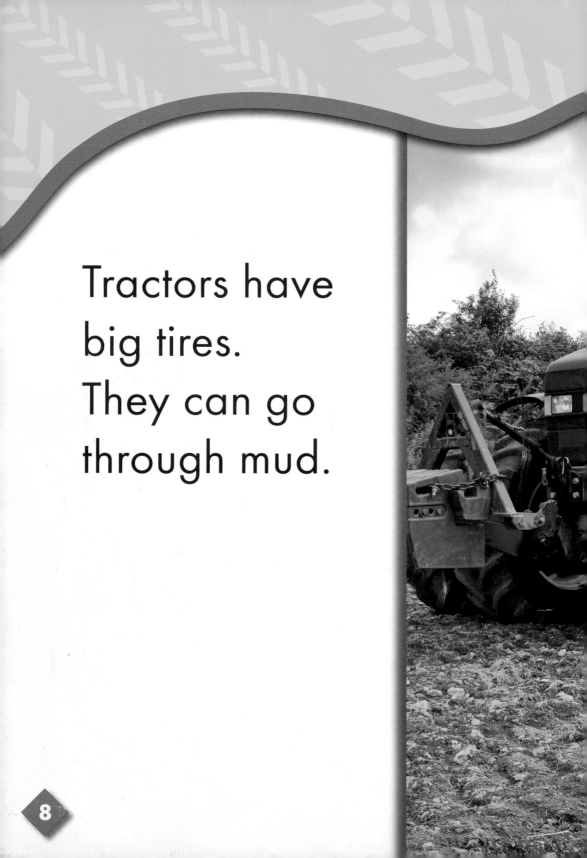

Tractors have
big tires.
They can go
through mud.

Some tractors have a **cab**. The driver sits in the cab.

A tractor has a **hitch**. A hitch hooks the tractor to machines that do many jobs.

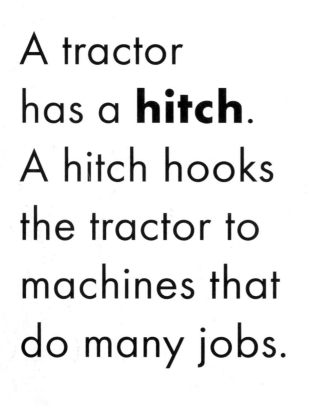

hitch

A tractor pulls a **plow**. A plow turns over the soil so farmers can plant seeds.

plow

A tractor pulls a **planter**. A planter puts seeds in the ground.

planter

A tractor pulls a **mower**. A mower cuts the grass.

mower

A tractor
starts a race.
Hang on!

Glossary

cab—a place for the driver to sit

hitch—the connection between a vehicle and a machine that the vehicle pulls behind it

mower—a machine that cuts down grass or plants

planter—a machine that plants seeds

plow—a machine that turns over soil to get it ready for planting

To Learn More

AT THE LIBRARY

Nelson, Kristin L. *Farm Tractors*. Minneapolis, Minn.: Lerner, 2002.

Tieck, Sarah. *Farm Tractors*. Edina, Minn.: ABDO, 2005.

Tractor. New York: DK Publishing, 2004.

ON THE WEB

Learning more about mighty machines is as easy as 1, 2, 3.

1. Go to www.factsurfer.com

2. Enter "mighty machines" into search box.

3. Click the "Surf" button and you will see a list of related web sites.

With factsurfer.com, finding more information is just a click away.

Index

The photographs in this book are reproduced through the courtesy of: Paul Prescott, front cover; Maurice van der Velden, p. 5; Chris Mellor/Getty Images, p. 7; texasmary, p. 9; Deere, Inc., pp. 11, 17, 19; Marek Pawluczuk, p. 13; Pixonet.com/Alamy, p. 15; Neil Phillip Mey, p. 21.

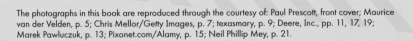